The Power of Human Energy

Unlock, Manage and Control the Energy That You Need

Kala Flynn

Published by powerofhumanenergy.com in 2018

powerofhumanenergy.com

ISBN 978-1-9996455-8-8

Illustrations by Richard Williams

The power of Human Energy is for all those who wish to make a friend of their life.

For all those who perceive the vague and distant shadows of a better way of being, where energies are under control.

For all those who have the courage to change.

About the Author

Born near Mount Kilimanjaro, educated and based in the UK, Kala Flynn has spent many years working as an accredited consultant in the field of personal development. Her specialties include corporate executive and business coaching, as well as organisational consulting and leadership development.

Kala's successful commercial career spans more than 20 years of working in senior board and executive roles within both global corporate and small organisations. Latterly she has operated as a trusted and sought-after independent consultant, helping individual clients, professionals and corporate management teams, learn how to direct their energies for more productive personal and business outcomes.

Kala is especially valued for the unique integrity, authenticity and accessibility of her approach, which is why she is able to establish long term relationships with her clients.

Kala now divides her time between professional coaching engagements, running masterclasses, workshops, speaking events and writing.

To contact the author and further resources please email; kala@powerofhumanenergy.com

What others have said…

"It is incredible that Kala has managed to bottle up over two decades of professional experience and observation in personal and professional energy into this easy to access book. A must read for all those who genuinely want to understand why they lack the energy they need and what to do about it"
Gary Adams. CEO, Healthcare Logistics Provider

"I have known Kala for over a decade, we have often discussed the subject of energy in its various guises and the way that it affects our attitude, the way we perform and our frame of reference. I am delighted that Kala has found the time to commit her thoughts into print to impart a deeper understanding of this fascinating subject."
Jeremy McNamara, COO, Global Research Company

"The Power of Human Energy by Kala Flynn is a book that can genuinely help people overcome the energy-draining effects of modern life. It is a wonderful new concept which has the power to help us in so many ways and understand why we lack the energy we need. The book serves as an excellent introduction to the subject of our Human Energy, covering a selective range of key and current topics, and leaving you hungry to find out more.. A must have, must read book"

Barbara Capstick, Specialist HR, Coach and Mediator

"Kala is one of the most experienced and highly qualified, innovative and creative executive leadership and development coaches in the UK. I am delighted that Kala has chosen to commit these thoughts to print and I can recommend this book to anyone who is curious about their energy and how to manage it"

C. Matcham CMgr FCMI, Managing Partner, Stewart Charles Associates

Acknowledgements

My gratitude goes out to all those who have given me continuous support in this idea, and who have provided me with the confidence and belief to embark on this work.

In particular I'd like to thank the 3 J's, my brother, the UCN and my father and mother for their unwavering belief in me and my ideas, and their relentless push to get this project started and finished.

I'd also like to extend a hearty thank-you to all my friends; my peers and associates for their support and warm and kind encouragement, emboldening me to push on and just get it done.

I have tested the concepts of the 3 core states with a professional sceptic and they have withstood the searing temperatures of our heated debates… thank you so much Professor for your infinite patience, intellectual guidance, for keeping it real and your help with this project.

Finally, I'd like to extend a special thank you to my coach who was sufficiently convinced of the need for this book that he was willing to eat his treasured Australian leather drover hat should time prove him wrong. I'm pleased to report that his hat remains intact.

December 2017 Kala Flynn

Contents

Introduction

I find the subject of Human Energy engrossing and compelling. After many years of working in the area of professional development, I have realised that Human Energy lies at the very core of the way we think, feel, behave and interact with the world. It is a subject much referred to in popular culture and yet, for the majority of people, it is a poorly defined concept that is rarely properly unpacked, examined and understood, especially in a first-person context.

Through my work in this area I have developed a subject speciality, distilling my ideas into a unique concept of three core energy states. This concept is designed to help people to understand more about their own Human Energy and to learn how to manage it to enhance and improve different aspects of their lives, in exactly the same way that I did, and continue to do.

In this book, I have attempted to synthesise this experience into an introductory guide. The subject is broad and deep and cannot be comprehensively covered in one small volume, so I have tried to focus on the basic ideas while hinting at further directions for exploration. As such this book should be regarded as a first primer on the subject.

Inevitably, in the course of writing, I have also discovered areas where I still need to develop enhanced personal energy-awareness, to continually recognise and refine my actions and 'practice what I preach'. I expect this process to continue indefinitely.

The things that people say...

I have sprinkled this book with carefully selected quotations from other authors. I have chosen their words because I find them a rich source of inspiration, and sometimes amusement, as I hope you will. I have also used them to hold up a mirror to the surrounding text, to offer an alternative space in which you can pause, take a moment to reflect and allow deeper layers of meaning and understanding to emerge in relation to the three core energy states.

Chapter 1

Human Energy Management

Most people are tired most of the time.

What's more, most people are tired of *being* tired, and many are searching for the magic elixir that will give them that little extra energy, that vital powerful edge.

One of the universal truths of our existence is the central importance of Human Energy. Our potential as individuals depends upon it. Human Energy is at the heart of everything we do.

My own personal journey has compelled me to ask some very searching questions about it. What I want to understand is:

- *What is our relationship with Human Energy?*
- *How do we absorb Human Energy and how do we transmit it to others?*
- *Can Human Energy be both good and bad for us, and how do we make use of the good and dissipate the bad?*
- *Do we use Human Energy wisely and with respect, or do we squander, reject, abuse or simply deny it?*
- *What drives our need, our search and our desire for more Human Energy?*

From everything I've seen and heard it seems to me that energy is easy to lose, but not so easy to gain.

More often than not people find their energy drained, not boosted, by those around them, be it their boss, team, spouse or partner, children, parent or friend. In addition, the very circumstances of our daily lives can be equally energy-depleting, examples including long working hours, lack of recognition, lack of job clarity and job security and not having a say in the home or work place.

In my continuing quest to map the landscape of Human Energy, I have sought to understand the nature of our different energy states and how they may be used and balanced for a better and more fulfilling life.

This quest has led me to the concept of the three core energy states, Power Down, Power Up and Power Through, which form the baseline of Human Energy management.

The true genesis of this book lay in a time of personal pain, fear and trauma, which led me to a moment of epiphany during which I realised just how important energy is, how much it means to me and how much it could mean to others.

Since that time many people, including my mentor, clients, family and friends, have encouraged me to share the insights I've gained from this experience. They felt that others may use these insights as tools to *unlock, manage and control* their own energy and make a positive difference to their lives and well-being.

This book is the first fruit of that effort.

To the reader new to these ideas, some of its contents may at first sound a little unconventional and unfamiliar. But I'm sure that the sense of what I'm saying will emerge as I share my experiences, ideas, research and explorations with you.

"You don't have to see the whole staircase to take the first step"

-Martin Luther King.

Chapter 2

Power Down - Power Up - Power Through

To start then, energy permeates our every move, thought and feeling. It weaves itself through our inner being and spills out into the world through our emotions, reactions, responses, decisions and behaviours.

Our energy is so significant to our existence that it even effects how we sleep, how we interact with others, and determines what filters we employ through which to see and interpret the world. Human Energy is our own personal currency... our currency for living.

And yet, so many people don't really get it. From moment to moment, most of us remain oblivious to the nature, requirements and impact of our own energy on ourselves and on others. At the same time, we are often unaware of how the energy of others impacts us. At best we may reflect on it after the event, but then only rarely and we are often left with no clear answer to the question..."why am I so tired?", "why am I so worn-out?".

This lack of consciousness is further compounded by energy displacement. We substitute what we really need with misguided desires. We expend energy in the rush towards the temporary satisfaction of something new or towards that thing, that place that makes us feel good.

This can lead us to unwittingly playing with our energy, challenging it, working against it and even pushing it beyond its limits. This is easy to do in a world that is changing at dizzying speed. The demands placed on us are relentless and overwhelming, constantly blind-siding us and calling for ever-increasing resources of cognitive, emotional, psychological and physical energy.

At what point do we learn to respect our energy? At what point do we learn that it is not our nemesis but our friend and constant companion?

In trying to answer these questions I have developed an insatiable curiosity about Human Energy.

Instead of just surviving in ignorance and missing out on what more life can be, with just a little more of the right type of energy, we can become active volunteers in our lives rather than mere conscripts.

Understanding this can help us to uncover the options, tools and ideas needed to influence and navigate our decisions and actions.

In other words, how do we use and profit from our energy currency?

The more I come to understand, the more questions open up. This is a broad, deep complex subject and it can't be covered in the space of just one book.

But we must begin somewhere...

So to share the first steps of my insights on Human Energy with you, I will be focussing in this book on what I have created and defined as the three core energy states.

We must understand these if we are to unlock, manage and control our Human Energy. This understanding must be practiced every day, every week, every month and every year if we are to be at our most creative and effective:

"The best investment you can make is an investment in yourself"

-Warren Buffet

So, what do the three core energy states look like?

The three core energy states

Power Down – In this state we consciously stop, breathe, switch-off and bring ourselves into a grounded position where we rejuvenate, recover and offload exhaustion. This is not a state of energy depletion, but one in which our energy is in a state of quiescence and stable equilibrium. It can be achieved through a variety of strategies including sleep, meditation, the use of colour or the completion of a challenging task. In the Power Down state, we are ready to Power Up.

Power Up – In this state we transform the calm, quiescent energy of the Power Down state into a raised dynamic state of high-energy potential, ready and available to be used to drive action. We achieve this transformation through activities or practices that have an energising effect on us. These can include listening to a favourite piece of music, taking a short burst of exercise, or the simple experience of having someone recognise and praise our work. In the high energy Power Up state we are ready to Power Through.

Power Through – In this state we use the dynamic energy from the Power Up state to maximum effect by converting it into directed physical, mental and emotional action. In the Power Through state, we deliver our best performance with the confidence that comes from high energy levels; smashing through tasks rather than merely surviving them. We deliver projects, run better quality meetings and achieve more in less time through the enhanced quality and focus deriving from abundant Human Energy.

These three energy states will form a common theme, a golden thread, running throughout this book, linking the thoughts and ideas contained within and pointing the way to enhanced well-being and a more productive way of life.

The time is NOW to unlock, manage and control your Human Energy.

Chapter 3

Mind and Possibilities

In July 2015 I fell suddenly ill, experiencing the most extreme and excruciating pain I'd ever known. I was rapidly admitted into the local Intensive Care Unit for emergency investigation. Within thirty minutes I was informed that, if I wanted to go home, there was no other choice but emergency surgery to resolve the issue.

I successfully underwent the operation under general anaesthetic. Later, during a post-op consultation, I was informed that I would not be provided with antibiotics or painkillers, since they might mask any adverse reactions, complications or relapses. I was also informed that as a consequence, my full recovery could be lengthy and uncomfortable, potentially taking up to twenty-four months. This was a battle I had not expected to fight and one I knew I had to find sufficient reserves of energy in order to win.

It was a shock I was not prepared for. I was left wondering "what just happened. What do I do now?" I have a loving family who are heavily reliant on me and my ability to keep on top of things. They maintain an unwavering belief in my having the energy to always be there for them. Furthermore, as an independent self-employed consultant my energy was entirely dependent upon my ability to continue working. I already had committed client engagements including scheduled meeting facilitations and a team development day set to take place in four weeks' time. I simply could not afford to let these go.

At this point I was confronted with a major crisis. I was faced with a fundamental disconnect between what the world said was true and what I *needed* to be true. I needed to be on my feet and fully functional again – and quickly, but I was in a highly energy-depleted state. My dilemma was further compounded by conflicting evidence. Others who had been through similar trauma told me to expect a long convalescence. On the other hand, my consultant felt that my general fitness and positive mind-set might support a more rapid recovery.

"There is nothing either good or bad but thinking makes it so"

-Shakespeare: Hamlet: Act 2, Scene 2

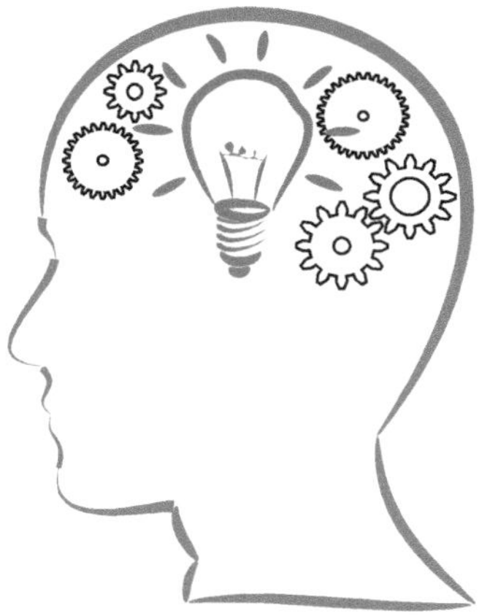

The consultant's optimistic view was all I needed to get started. I realised that a rapid recovery would require a great deal of commitment and *energy* – physical, mental and emotional. But at this point energy was the one commodity in dangerously short supply. I knew that blindly throwing myself into a recovery effort would most likely drain what little energy I had left and only serve to make my situation worse. What I needed first was to place myself into a comfortable and stable state where I would be ready to energise myself for the struggle ahead. I realised I needed to take control, manage my personal energy and Power Down before I could Power Up!

"In the midst of winter, I found there was, within me, an invincible summer. And that makes me happy. For it says that no matter how hard the world pushes against me, within me, there's something stronger – something better, pushing right back"

-Albert Camus

This was a new way of thinking for me, but necessity is the mother of invention. I refused to accept the stated terms of my recovery and decided to reject any self-limiting beliefs.

"Life is 10% of what happens to you but 90% of how you react to it"

-Charles Swindle

Human Energy is your capacity to change. It transforms your values and beliefs into resilient behaviour. High energy increases your freedom to use your Human Energy constructively and improves your ability to respond to stress, illness and trauma.

I would place my personal energy at the centre of my recovery strategy and become the subject of my own investigation. It would be an exercise in self-control and self-belief. Firstly, I set an ambitious recovery target of thirty days. This may seem recklessly aggressive, but I really needed to master this one!

Next, I set about building my resistance and healing energy. Antibiotics and painkillers were ruled out, and I felt that this was no bad thing, since I have never been a believer in their excessive levels of use in modern society. Instead I looked towards alternative treatments combined with sound practical advice to take lots of rest and regular meals, sprinkled with healthy doses of self-compassion. In this strategy, I was blessed by having a consultant who was open to this hybrid approach.

Like conventional medicine, alternative treatments have their rules of application, and these must be understood and followed for best effect. For example, I disciplined myself to stop drinking coffee, which negated the effects of some of my treatments, and replaced it with green tea which is more efficacious. I was fortunate that green tea was allowed, as I had discovered its energy benefits some time earlier.

Through these means I was able to move to a state of energy equilibrium, a state in which my psychological, emotional and physical energies became calm, stabilised and in harmony. I had Powered Down, not by dissipating and wasting my energies in misdirected and futile efforts, but by carefully husbanding them, supporting them through sympathetic medication and rest, so that I was quickly ready to re-energise and Power Up to recovery.

Within thirty days, I was back to a fully functional state without any deleterious effects. I met my recovery target!

A key lesson that I learned from this experience is that positive or negative states of mind can produce positive or negative physiological effects in the body. The importance of Power Down, Power Up and Power Through is not confined to the realm of the psychological, but can also have a profound influence on the realm of the physical.

This fact manifests itself in many different ways, but perhaps most importantly in the phenomenon of sleep.

Chapter 4

Sleep and the Art of Powering Down

I used to hate sleep. I considered it a complete waste of time, an inconvenience. I used to think that sleep was for those who had no sense of the urgency and vitality of life. This may sound strange but to me the very thought of sleep was anathema.

Sleep represented loss of the precious commodity of time, time that I could be using for active creative work and productive living. Life, after all, is not a rehearsal for the show, it *is* the show, and every minute is irretrievable, it's not coming back.

My appetite for life, my drive and determination all fuelled my ideas and creativity. The more the ideas flowed and the more enthusiastic I became, the more

I rejected the very concept of sleep. This irrationality was compounded by the fact that I also associated too much sleep with laziness, procrastination and the fear of physical and psychological deterioration.

I inhabited a belief system that created an inwardly spiralling vicious cycle in which I would continually compete with myself to get by on as little sleep as possible. This generated its own addictive brand of energy, a kind of insomniac euphoria, similar to the high experienced by the exercise junky, addicted to the Gym. However, inside I knew that this state of affairs could not continue indefinitely. I needed to examine my belief system and reconfigure my relationship with sleep.

"To the believer no proof is necessary, to the non-believer, no proof is ever enough"

-Thomas Aquinas

Beliefs can be held without justification, but with sufficient justification beliefs become knowledge.

Without the solid support of adequate justification however, beliefs must support themselves by means of their own energy. This energy, refracted through the prism of our beliefs, drives our actions.

My actions, being driven by the energy of my beliefs about sleep, were self-destructive and energy-depleting. This realisation was finally forced upon me during my recovery. At that time, I needed to safely Power Down if I was to stand any chance of *quickly* Powering Up.

Rest, including sleep, was an integral part of that process. I came to realise, recognise and reframe the value of sleep.

I could not continue as before, so I changed my belief.

As part of this change I also came to see that it was not the mere *quantity* of sleep that counted so much as the *quality*. You can sleep for ten to fourteen hours or more and still feel lousy upon waking, and sluggish for the rest of the day. On the other hand, you can sleep for six to eight hours and feel refreshed, rejuvenated and ready to go....

But how do we achieve the quality sleep that will enable us to Power Down? Research shows that we experience several phases of nightly sleep, and to some extent all of these are necessary for delivering high quality rest. However there is one phase which is particularly important, and this is Rapid Eye Movement (REM) sleep.

REM sleep is a phase of our sleep pattern characterised by rapid movement of the eyes, low muscle tone and a propensity to dream. It occurs periodically during our nightly ninety-minute sleep cycles. Its precise function remains unknown, although there is evidence that it plays a role in memory consolidation, mood regulation and our ability to reason.

What we do know is that, with the exception of certain clinical conditions such as depression, REM sleep is a highly rejuvenating sleep phase. If we are deprived of it we show severe behavioural and physiological anomalies. Clearly REM sleep is essential to our well-being and a balanced energy state. Without adequate REM sleep we are unlikely to be able to Power Down. Aiming for high quality sleep should therefore be a daily goal.

Of course, all this assumes that we have a lifestyle structured to support such good intentions. In our smart, slick modern lives, this is increasingly difficult to achieve.

We are slowly but inexorably becoming bound up in a twenty-four hour world where the demands of commerce and consumption, the pressure of 'always on' personal communications and our obligations to service the needs of others, never themselves seem to sleep.

We dare not switch off our devices in case missing that next call, text or email would bring on some imagined commercial or social disaster. We fear becoming cut off and 'out of the loop'. This fear has even been given its own name – fear of missing out (FOMO). Our working day now extends from the moment we wake to the moment we fall asleep, because it can. We even take our phones to bed and fail to switch them off! We become accomplices in our own exhaustion.

Time, through its physical surrogate the clock, becomes our enemy. Our anxiety mounts. We look to dispense with everything that is unproductive and therefore unnecessary, and we increasingly come to see sleep time as an irritation, a dispensable commodity. Just as I once did.

Here are some questions you may wish to consider about your relationship with sleep:

> *Q: How important is sleep to you?*
>
> *Q: Do you wake in the morning feeling refreshed and energetic or sluggish and drowsy?*
>
> *Q: How often do you find it hard to get to sleep?*
>
> *Q: What is the impact of poor quality sleep?*

Q: What strategies could you employ to achieve good quality sleep?

The emotional drain that anxiety creates when we constantly feel that we're "up against the clock" is debilitating and disruptive. It impairs our ability to think clearly and impacts how we articulate our message to others.

Being time-poor is not the only factor that can leave us emotionally exhausted with no space to Power Down or Power Up. To the list of modern ills we can also add new kinds of social pressures, stress, relationship anxiety and financial hardships. The list is practically endless.

So how can we step out of this vicious cycle and ensure we get the high quality sleep that will truly power us down? I managed it through the necessity of recovery from illness. However, everyone's circumstances are different. There are no 'magic bullets', but there are a few simple and basic guidelines that may help.

Firstly, we can decide to adopt a regular schedule, going to sleep and waking at roughly the same time every day, and ensuring we have around seven to nine hours sleep per night.

Next, we can avoid stimulants such as caffeine, alcohol, dark chocolate and carbonated soft drinks in the hours before we sleep, as well as turning off other stimulating and addictive distractions such as computers, tablets and smart phones, and wherever possible, leaving them outside the bedroom. Finally, we can ensure that our sleep environment is cool, dark and quiet.

These guidelines are fine as far as they go, but there are also additional things we can do, habits we can adopt, to help us switch out of the energy draining mode and into the state where we're ready to Power Down and prepare ourselves to Power Up.

Chapter 5

Cooking Up a Storm of Inner Calm

For those of us who suffer from smart gadget addiction and simply refuse to be parted from our phones, tablets or laptops, there is always the possibility of redemption. We can turn our dependency into a virtue by enlisting our gadgets in helping us achieve the desired state in preparation for a good nights' sleep. For example, we can use guided meditation or play sleep music or white noise, which can be easily found on-line or as simple downloadable Apps.

For those of us who are mercifully free of gadget addiction, there are other means of achieving a good night's sleep. Preliminary research suggests that writing down a to-do list of the tasks that you will need to complete tomorrow may have positive sleep benefits.

My personal favourite tool for Powering Down is the daily gratitude journal, although some people may prefer to refer to it as a diary. I generally use it in the evening but it can be used at other times of the day as an effective means of achieving a grounded state in readiness for Powering Up.

We may not always *feel* grateful. Being grateful even when you're not may seem artificial, awkward or arduous. It could even feel insincere. However, it is actually a powerful tool that can be directed towards constructive purposes, and its benefits are rooted in objective fact. Your brain cannot feel glum and grateful at the same time.

According to research published in the Cerebral Cortex Journal (Feb 2009; 19(2): 276-283) gratitude stimulates the hypothalamus which in turn stimulates the ventral tegmental area of our brain – the 'reward circuitry' or 'bliss centre' that produces the sensation of pleasure.

It is empirical science – but it's also common sense, focussing on good things makes you feel better than focussing on the bad.

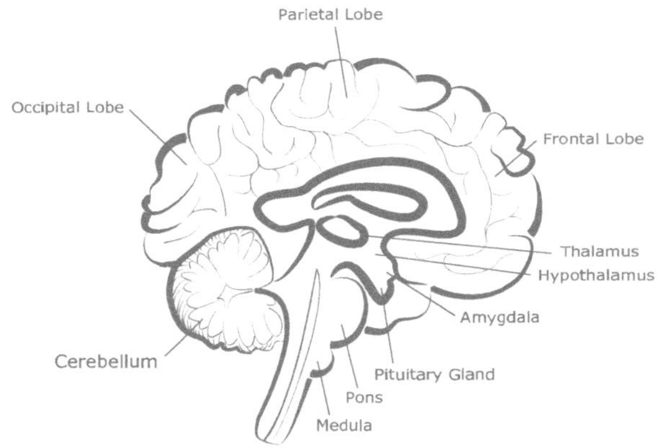

"He is a man of sense that does not grieve for what he has not, but rejoices in what he has"

-Epictetus

When you possess a high level of gratitude, you often feel an open sense of wonder, thankfulness and appreciation of life itself. *I know I did!*

Researchers are finding that people who exhibit and express the most gratitude are happier, healthier and more energetic. They report fewer symptoms of aches and pains such as headaches. They also feel less lonely, less stressed, less anxious and less depressed. *I can personally vouch for that too!*

Reports show that using a gratitude journal every night can also dramatically improve your quality of sleep and you wake up with a happier, more resourceful mind-set.

I have continued with the daily gratitude journal and I'm happy to confess that I'm quite addicted to it. In sharing this with you I hope you will be encouraged to practice this yourself and enjoy the benefits that will flow from it.

It's a simple three step process:

Step 1 – *you need to create a journal. The format doesn't matter. Ideally it should be paper and pen, a diary, or a notebook. For the gadget-dependent it could even be a PC, tablet or smartphone. The point is it needs to be something that is constantly accessible to you.*

Step 2 – *make a new entry in your journal for each day. Write down what you are grateful for, what positive things happened today and what things you may be thankful for tomorrow. Aim for three to five things.*

Step 3 – *Repeat step 2 daily. Keep the journal by your side and refer to it. This is especially empowering during those challenging times when we experience particularly low and negative moments. This practice puts you into the energy state that refuels, rejuvenates and repairs. It naturally lifts you* *to a subtle sense of implicit inner calm from which you can easily Power Down.*

Gratitude is a *very* powerful tool and really does help to dramatically change things for the better. It can make you more effective and generate a greater sense of calm, control and composure.

"None is more impoverished than the one who has no gratitude. Gratitude is a currency that we can mint for ourselves and spend without fear of bankruptcy"

-Fred De Witt Van Amburgh

There are other ways that we can employ gratitude, as well as through our personal journals. In addition to building our own resources, choosing gratitude as a way of being, can also elevate those around us.

This is where Powering Up can manifest itself through the gratitude we give and receive from others. For example, a simple "thank you", or show of appreciation when we give way to others in traffic, costs nothing but goes a long, long way to making both parties feel good about a kindly gesture. Wouldn't it be interesting if gratitude became embedded in our behaviour as every day 'business as usual'?

Research from the University of Southern California *(Journal of Experimental Social Psychology, Volume 48, Issue 3, May 2012, 778-782),* underlines the fact that gratitude can have positive Power Up benefits during every day activities. It showed that in the workplace the practice of gratitude can remove conflict from interpersonal interactions.

The best way to counter aggression and anger is with a heart-felt "thank you".

Where we feel a storm brewing, gratitude is a key tool for creating an eye of inner calm at its centre and helping those around us to Power Up and Power Down.

"Gratitude is the healthiest of all human emotions"

-Zig Ziglar

Chapter 6

Tired of Being Tired

Why do we often feel more energetic at 11 in the evening than we do when we wake at 6 in the morning?

Surely, after a good night's rest should we not be fully refreshed and ready to go? Ready to hop out of bed, rush out of the house and into the car to get to work, or jump on the train to get to that all-important meeting? But often we feel drained, lethargic and unwilling to move. It takes us time to warm up from a sluggish start and we feel that we simply can't function until we've had that first coffee, that first caffeine hit of the day.

One reason is that, right up until the moment we go to sleep, we keep our brains active rather than preparing to Power Down. As a result, during the night we don't get the high quality sleep we need. We don't Power Down, we simply expend energy. When the morning comes we are in no fit shape to Power Up. The lights are on, the eyes are open but there's no-one home, as the vacant expression testifies.

So, when there is no Power Down, what happens to us? All too frequently the answer is we enter a repeating cycle of tiredness.

This is a common feeling. The Royal College of Psychiatrists has reported that one in ten of us feels permanently fatigued, while one in five reports feeling unusually tired at any one time. Similarly, according to a recent survey of General Practitioners in the UK *(BBC Focus, October 2017)*, 20% of patient consultations are about tiredness. This new epidemic has prompted GPs to start using the acronym TATT *(Tired All The Time)* in their consultation notes. Around 5% of patients visiting their GP complain of TATT and half will be given a diagnosis of 'stress'.

Tiredness now seems to be an endemic feature of our world, and modern life has found many ways to trigger it.

Poor diet, as a direct result of a hectic lifestyle, is a major contributor to the problem:

- We frequently skip meals such as breakfast because our time is hijacked by a constant stream of external demands and our crazy rush to get out of the door.
- We live on fast foods loaded with sugar and simple carbohydrates, giving us regular spikes in our blood sugar levels, followed by sharp

drops, causing metabolic stress, leaving us fatigued.

- We tend to drink too little water leading to energy-draining fluid loss, while relying on excessive use of caffeine and alcohol as artificial stimulants, particularly in the evenings before we sleep.
- Often, we don't replenish the iron in our blood, starving our tissues of oxygen and denying them the energy they need.

The hectic lifestyle also drives poor living and working habits which further deplete our energy:

- Social jet lag – late nights and morning lie-ins – disrupt our body's natural timed rhythms which govern sleep and wakefulness.
- Working and travelling long hours, weekends and even holidays under pressure of deadlines, combined with an inability to say "No" to escalating workloads, affords no

opportunity to Power Down, Power Up or Power Through.

- Perfectionism, an absence of a sense of self satisfaction in our work, worry, anxiety, depression and boredom all sap our will and strength, rendering us impotent to properly manage our energy states.
- Tiredness itself drives us to skip the regular exercise that we would normally use as an enabler to Power Down or Power Up. This in turn has a negative physical effect, increasing our feelings of exhaustion, lowering our general level of health and sometimes leading to bouts of low mood.

Endemic tiredness, if left unaddressed, will seriously diminish our quality of life and take a heavy mental and physical toll. Research indicates that it can significantly lower our immune resistance, making us vulnerable to recurrent infections. Research also suggests that it can increase the risk of obesity, heart disease, diabetes and stroke. When we're tired it is harder for us to stay positive and optimistic, increasing our feelings of lethargy, fatigue, stress and anxiety.

This is quite a bundle of issues. We may know we feel tired all the time, but few of us have any clear idea why or what we should do about it. Almost invariably we reach for a quick fix, some magic bullet that will get us up on our feet again. This usually takes the form of an artificial stimulant, something that will remove the problem, energise us and make us feel better, if only for long enough to let us do our job and manage our obligations.

The fix could be some off-the-shelf medication, or one or more of the old stand-by solutions - caffeine, alcohol or worse. But there is a fundamental misconception at the heart of this strategy.

Applying artificial sedatives is NOT the same as Powering Down.

Applying artificial stimulants is NOT the same as Powering Up.

Operating in a stimulant-induced high energy state is NOT the same as Powering Through.

When you reach for that triple expresso on the way to the meeting, or that extra glass of wine in the evening while you struggle to finish tomorrow morning's presentation, you are merely applying a band aid to the problem. Once the artificial stimulus is removed, or wears off, there is nothing to fall back on and your energy takes a nose-dive, or crashes completely, leaving you feeling worse than before and ready for another band aid.

"The only way to keep your health is to eat what you don't want, drink what you don't like and do what you'd rather not"

-Mark Twain

So how do we escape the tiredness trap?

To address the problem we need to learn how to manage our Human Energy through the three core states of Power Down, Power Up and Power Through. In order to manage and control our tiredness we must learn how to employ all three core energy states, not necessarily at the same time, but always in harmony, producing a virtuous cycle from which new capabilities emerge and the whole becomes greater than the sum of its parts.

But what does this mean for the individual? We are all unique, and how we Power Down, Power Up and Power Through will be different for each person.

A universal and natural means of Powering Down is sleep, which I have already discussed in an earlier chapter. Good quality sleep is a highly restorative process during which your body and mind undergo a re-set, and potentiate themselves for Powering Up on waking. When we awake from a good sleep or a power nap, things often seem much clearer and our thoughts and ideas seem to flow more easily. That hasty late night email or text sent in the heat of stress, may be regretted in the clear light of the morning. When I was a child and life seemed particularly challenging my grandparents often used to say "why don't you stay calm and sleep on it? Things will sort themselves out and all will seem fine in the morning". *More often than not they did.*

Sleep is a passive way of Powering Down, but some individuals may prefer to Power Down by actively expending energy. At first this may seem like a contradiction, but remember, Powering Down is not the same as energy depletion, tiredness or fatigue. In the Power Down state we have not lost energy. We have brought our energy into a calm, marshalled and harmonious state from which we can naturally power up without the aid of artificial stimulation.

Expending energy to Power Down may involve physical exercise such as going for a walk or a stroll.

Energy makes energy. The mere act of going for a brisk walk can help you deal with the tiredness brought on by social jet-lag, lack of physical exercise or just plain boredom. It can also cure the 'cabin fever' resulting from being cooped up in an office or at home all day, a little like being trapped inside a Tupperware box. In addition, it can create an enhanced feeling of well-being, through the natural production of serotonin.

The Power Down effect of physical exercise is not new, but has been known in one form or another for millennia. It's one example of the benefits of an abrupt change of activity, also referred to as 'breaking state'. When you reach a point of exhaustion in one activity, it is often highly beneficial to break state and get up and go and do something completely unconnected.

The new activity may not involve any conscious thinking, or it may require a switch of intellectual focus, such as carpentry, listening to a favourite piece of music, reading a novel or doing the ironing. A familiar example of where breaking state can be beneficial is 'writer's block'. Writers suffer from a kind of word-exhaustion, where no matter how hard they try, the words simply will not come.

History is replete with stories of light-bulb moments experienced while breaking state. Perhaps one of the most famous is the story of Archimedes' principle which he is reputed to have hit upon while taking a bath.

It is clear that while we may have refocussed our conscious activity, our unconscious mind is still working on the problem. So instead of reaching for the coffee pot, break state, take time out, go for a walk, try a little gardening, or have a conversation on some unrelated topic with a friend.

The three core energy states are closely linked and one person's Powering Down may be another's person's Powering Up. Taking the right kind of exercise or listening to the right kind of music may also serve to get you Powered Up to Power Through. The particular activity you choose and how you use it depends on your personal preferences and what you need from your Human Energy management.

If you are tired of being tired, it's time to start developing your own personal strategies for using the three core states to drive a rejuvenated, revitalised and more productive life.

"I am smiled out, talked out, quipped out, socialised so far from any being, I need the moral silences to get realised back to myself"

-John Ciardi

Chapter 7

Denial – In the Service of Delusions

Consistently low energy levels and a state of feeling constantly drained may be our body's way of signaling that something is under serious stress and needs attention, healing or rejuvenation. Worse still, it may mean that something is actually damaged or broken and possibly in need of medical intervention.

But many people often remain in a state of *denial.*

Sometimes we're just too close to see the wood for the trees and instead of taking remedial action, we simply try to cope by taking on subliminal tasks that distract our attention without requiring engagement in thought. Activities that often fall into this category include house cleaning, polishing the car or randomly surfing the Internet. It's important to understand that this is not a form of breaking state in order to manage your energy, it's a form of denial and displacement – an attempt to run away.

In addition the coping strategies we adopt can often compound the problem, creating unhelpful behavioral side effects such as overworking, insomnia and various forms of active and passive aggression. They may also lead to eating irregularities including loss of appetite or, at the other extreme, cravings and binging.

In these instances taking a little time to breathe, reflect, re-connect with our core values and reclaim our sense of self can be helpful and liberating. In this space we have the potential to access and manage our three core states of Power Down, Power Up and Power Through. However all too often this is too hard or too frightening to do. Most people will not go there, and certainly not without some external assistance such as coaching, mentoring or counseling. For some people even this form of help is a ‘bridge too far’.

The fact is that we are more strangers to ourselves than we are to other people. We are more easily persuaded by ourselves than by others, and we are certainly the easiest person to fool. We tell ourselves comfortable lies instead of facing the issues, and in so doing can deny ourselves the right to a healthier and happier life.

Denial comes in many different flavours. Some wait to be rescued, hoping someone else will take on the responsibility of doing the thinking. Thinking is hard. It consumes a disproportionate amount of our energy, which is probably why most people take great pains to avoid it. All too often, rescue never comes.

"Most people would rather die than think and many of them do!"

-Bertrand Russell

For others the idea that they may need help at all feels like a sign of weakness, a sign of 'giving in'. They would rather soldier on and maintain a stiff upper lip than admit their need and reach out to work with others for a mutually energising solution. How many times have you said, or heard someone else say "I find other people so pedestrian, they just slow me down!", or "by the time I've explained it I may as well have done it myself"?

Another denial strategy is to waste time in the Assume Room, where things are subject to constant misinterpretation and misunderstanding. When we make an assumption we are effectively forming an opinion, we are willfully accepting a proposition about the world without checking for the evidence. We believe what we *want* to believe, we assume we *know*, when in reality we should be getting to the truth of things through conversation, exploration and understanding with others. It is worth noting that understanding does not imply agreement. We can understand something without necessarily agreeing that it's true. With assumptions we tend to over-think, catastrophise and blow things out of proportion.

"In the service of delusions we drain our energy, and the energy of those around us"

Meanwhile it may seem to us that we are Powered Up and using our energy constructively, but of course this is illusory.

A friend of mine has a sister who is a permanent resident of the Assume Room. Raised in a dysfunctional family environment, she grew to adulthood assuming that life will always be a negative experience, that the small, insignificant incidents that form the fabric of her daily life are in reality hiding a catastrophe. She finds it hard to deal with the most mundane problem, always over-reacting, assuming the worst, and burning energy in stratagems that are at best unnecessary and at worst actually damaging to herself and to others. This infects those around her, who are quickly recruited into joining her in the Assume Room. It's hard to be more than an hour in her company before feeling drained of energy.

Unsurprisingly, her constant mantra is how tired and fatigued she always feels.

"Assumptions make a slave of Human Energy"

Denial is fueled by the fear of facing what we perceive to be an unpleasant reality. This fear may prohibit us from taking action, from engaging in activities which we find challenging and even frightening. For some this may be fear of speaking in public. For others it may be fear of changing jobs or boarding a plane.

Instead of taking up the challenge we prefer to stay in our comfort zone, to remain with the familiar. We deny our capabilities and tell ourselves "Oh I could never do that". Worse still we may excuse ourselves by denying that we even want or need to take the risk; "I'm just fine as I am thank you".

"The cave you fear to enter holds the treasure you seek"

-Joseph Campbell

All of these denial strategies have something in common. They represent a fear of taking full responsibility for ourselves and ownership of our own lives.

"Denial prevents us from harnessing our Human Energy"

This fear often results in displacement activities – an attempt to run away from the real issues. Some may retreat to a private space – for men it may be their 'Man Cave'. Others may take refuge in the anaesthetic of a stiff drink. Alternatively, the displacement may take the form of stonewalling or simply not responding or reacting. Sometimes people may busy themselves in conversations focused on other people's problems and anxieties. They may take comfort from the sugar rush of a fancy cake, or indulge in retail therapy in an attempt to reclaim or reinvent themselves.

"A life lived in fear is a life half lived"

-Spanish proverb

But in reality, there is nothing to be afraid of. We can use the three core states as a path to transforming our denial strategies into something more virtuous and empowering.

Choosing not to run away, but temporarily remaining within our comfort zone, need not be a refuge taken in fear, a cop-out or a low energy dead-end. Instead we can choose to see it as a stress-free space where we can marshal our energy, take the time to reflect at our own pace and allow ourselves to look the demon in the eye, examine the thing we are denying, the source of our fear. We may even take the opportunity to reach out to others for exploration, advice and a new perspective.

In so doing we will enter a Power Down state where we are no longer spending our energy in an attempt to escape, but have slowly gained the energy to look forward towards new possibilities. We begin to take back control of our lives. We are now in a good place from which to Power Up.

Attempting to do the thing we fear can be intimidating and frightening. However, if we have Powered Down, then we have set the scene for a potentially rewarding experiment. Often, we find that the experience we feared can be highly energising, actually allowing us to Power Up in the process and reveal new capabilities we didn't know we had.

The fearful person who stands up before a crowded auditorium to speak on a subject they care about will frequently find they grow wings. The subject and their speech take on a life of their own, and they leave the fear on the ground far below them.

Appreciation from the audience will also reinforce the Power Up effect and soon they will be Powering Through. Afterwards, they may even ask themselves "is *this* what I was afraid of?"

"Come to the edge," he said.

"We can't, we're afraid!" they responded.

"Come to the edge," he said.

"We can't, we will fall!" they responded.

"Come to the edge," he said.

And so they came.

And he pushed them.

And they flew."

-Guillaume Apollinaire

Those who inhabit the Assume Room where they concoct their own version of reality can also benefit from transforming their denial into more constructive thinking. The denial that drives assumptions is no different from any other, and can be dealt with in the same way. This will also liberate those who have been unwillingly recruited into the Assume Room.

Placing ourselves within a constructive thinking space gives us the opportunity to energetically access our three core states, beginning with Power

Down, which then provides us with the potential to Power Up, ready to Power Through. We give ourselves the chance to escape, and find the room to take a step back or step aside from our fears. We see them through a new lens and within a wider context, and finally reclaim the sense of self that we had lost through the unintentional trap of denial.

"It's not denial.

I'm just selective about the reality I accept"
-Bill Watterson

Chapter 8

The Personal Power Gym

"Until you have done something for humanity you should be ashamed to die"

-Horace Mann

See the potential within others and act with maturity, integrity and compassion.

When we meet others with intelligence, openness, integrity and a sense of compassion we give and receive a different kind of energy, an energy which communicates authenticity. We gain a different perspective and become more open to seeing positive intentions behind their actions. Our relational interplay with others can become more collaborative and productive interactions often emerge. Sometimes it's just a question of stepping aside and letting our open and authentic self listen and speak on our behalf.

This is a natural approach which I endeavour to adopt in all my personal and professional interactions, my small and local contribution to the elevation of the human state.

There is an old saying that it takes more energy to frown than to smile. The scientific truth of this is debatable, but the underlying message is clear – emotions are infectious and when you smile, the world does indeed smile with you.

But for most of us, most of the time, this is hard to do. We are so often caught up in the imperatives of everyday life, taking care of business and getting through the day. We move through the world in a semi-detached way, the next task becomes the driver and we don't notice most of what's around us.

This is especially true when times get seriously tough and we're under major stress. Our problems can seem overwhelming and all-consuming, blocking our ability to see the good in things. We walk around with a heavy heart, our breathing becomes shallow and we feel a sense of helplessness and despair.

I know from personal experience what this feels, smells and sounds like, but it's not so easy to know how we appear to others at times like these. How we perceive ourselves is often quite different from how others perceive us. It's often the case that others will sense that there is something wrong by the energy we are transmitting, long before we are able to admit it to ourselves. While recovering from my illness my family were often able to see when I needed to Power Down even before I was aware of it.

You can tell more about a person from their energy than their words.

When we're burning out, others will notice it first because it leaks out in all sorts of ways. We may try to hide our inner struggle to cope with the sheer pace of our lives, but we will betray our exhaustion in the tonality and articulation of our speech. What we say is different from what we intend to say because our mental attention and focus become diluted or exhausted by multiple competing distractions.

Amongst all this busy cacophony we struggle and strive to take care of all kinds of business except the one that really matters – ourselves. We consistently fail to take the time to Power Down, to relax, to breathe, to be open, awake and present. This state of affairs becomes familiar to everyone at some point in their lives.

But if we are to live well in the modern world and continue to thrive, what is to be done?

For some help we can turn to the concept of the 'Personal Power Gym'.

I took a phone-call from a close friend recently and when I asked how he was doing he replied, "oh not bad, keeping alive – you know". I clearly sensed by the tone of his voice that things were probably quite difficult and that he was struggling to keep on top of all the demands that the world was making of him.

Curious to know more, I asked, "what's all the stress about right now and how are you responding to it?" I knew full well that he was more likely reacting than responding and I wondered to myself when he had last been in a Power Down state and able to properly Power Up.

He replied, "Everyone just wants a piece of me and I can't spread myself any thinner. Everyone thinks their stuff is crucial, important or urgent. But when I think about it my stuff is critical and urgent too! It just gets to a point where I feel overloaded with it all and I can't think to how make sense of things or to plan things out!

He then added, "It feels horrendous, but then when I start to think that their problems are NOT urgent, are NOT a matter of life and death, I start to feel guilty!"

He was right of course. In reality people's problems are rarely a matter of life and death. But knowing this does not help when your sense of obligation and guilt places you in the middle of the deep blue ocean, with no life raft and no sense of how you will escape your predicament. It becomes a matter of psychological survival.

As the conversation continued he mentioned that he regularly engaged in altruistic activities – things he did for others which brought him great enjoyment. It was his way of coping with the stress, his way of

Powering Down to Power Up. Unfortunately this sometimes brought with it the feeling that indulging himself in this way was selfish. This caused him more feelings of guilt which in turn further depleted his energy!

I pointed out to him that guilt is an unconscious response to values being compromised. But whose values were being compromised here? The time he donates to his philanthropic activities provides happiness to others, it lights up their lives and gives them connection, hope and something to look forward to. How could this be a reason for guilt?

He thought this over and replied, "I do feel it's important that so many people get so much from it. I guess the problem is the time I have to take out of my day to do it. When I get back to base I find the tasks, chores and demands are still there and stacking up! It just drains my energy. I feel like I'm firefighting and I just can't move".

"There is not enough time to do all the nothing we want to do"

-Bill Watterson

At this point a potent new idea took shape in my mind. "Ok, how about if you looked at your altruistic activities as your own Personal Power Gym. I don't mean the gym, I mean the Personal Power Gym?"

I was not actually referring to a conventional gym. I was referring to the gym that resides in the realm of the abstract. This realm is the place where conceptual activities offer us the opportunity to deliberately move into a new mind-set.

The Personal Power Gym can incorporate activities such as the mind gym, the humour gym, the music gym, or the movie gym. I was describing an activity that gives us a moment to break state and take a paradigm shift! When we visit the Personal Power Gym we take time out to personally repair, refresh and access our three core states. A ten minute work-out gives us a little time and space to disengage from the energy-draining pressures of every-day life and to re-focus. It provides us with an opportunity to step back, re-energise, Power Down and Power Up for fresh impetus to get on with the tasks in hand.

The Personal Power Gym can take many different forms, depending on individual preferences and needs. We may choose to listen to some calming music to help us Power Down, or more up-beat music to energise and Power us Up. Laughter is also a very potent way of Powering Down or Powering Up. Indeed, laughter is used in some forms of therapy. Taking time to cook a favourite meal provides us with an opportunity to re-focus our attention, let go of anxieties and allow our senses of vision, smell and taste to help Power Up our creative energy.

Just as with a physical gym, the function of the Personal Power Gym is to give us time to attend to our own health and well-being, to manage our Human Energy and put us back on track. It's all about using the three core states, and at any given time you can choose the particular Gym that best evokes the state you need to be in. It's even possible to use the Gym to achieve more than one state. A good example is the problem of clutter.

We all know the scenario. The flotsam and jetsam that steadily wash up on the shores of our lives can sometimes become overwhelming.

At first it's just part of the background, but get past a certain point and clutter can start to be a serious drain on your energy. You look at it every day and it stares right back at you as if to say "I'm still here and if you ignore me I'm just going to get worse. What are you going to do about it?"

We turn away pretending we haven't heard, but this silent challenge soon becomes deafening, and the louder it becomes, the more energy we drain in resisting it.

There are many reasons why we accumulate clutter. Perhaps we are naturally disorganised. Perhaps we are lazy, or perhaps we convince ourselves that these things may come in useful later, while knowing deep down we'll almost certainly never need them again.

"If I won the award for laziness, I would send someone to pick it up for me"

-Unknown

Quite often, blinding ourselves to clutter represents an avoidance of something we find hard to deal with, such as the death of a loved one. This plays on our deepest emotions and is especially energy-draining - another form of denial.

When we decide to de-clutter we are entering the Personal Power Gym to plug a hole through which our Human Energy is steadily leaking. It can be a metaphor for our life. We begin to take control of those things that continually nag at us, and we jettison them by an act of resolute commitment, an act of letting go.

"Not till we are lost . . . do we begin to find ourselves"

-Henry David Thoreau

It's a liberating way of Powering Down, but also of Powering Up and Powering Through as we remove the noise and emerge into a quieter, more peaceful and organised world, a world which perhaps we can begin to see through the lens of integrity, openness and authenticity.

Chapter 9

Multi-Sense and Sensibility

"No idea is conceived in our mind independent of our five senses"

-Albert Einstein

We are all connected to the world via our senses. All the information we have and everything we understand about the world comes via these few restricted channels. It's little wonder then that our senses can profoundly affect our emotions, our creativity and our Human Energy.

Vision

A friend of mine loves art. He's very fond of the Dutch Masters and particularly the work of Johannes Vermeer. While attending a conference in Holland one year, he decided to take an impromptu excursion to The Hague to view the one Vermeer painting he had not yet seen, the Girl with a Pearl Earring. Sometimes called the Mona Lisa of the north, the identity of the girl in the picture has long been disputed and has even formed the subject of a major movie.

Standing before the painting he was transfixed by the composition, the way her head is turning to glance back at the observer, the use of light to create the softness of the skin on her face and highlight the moisture in her eyes and on her lips. There was a sense of energy radiating from the picture. But mostly he was astonished at the way the artist had visually captured the essence of the person herself. He felt as if he were looking at this girl through the living eyes of a man who had been dead for 330 years. He felt he could know

what she was thinking, that he could talk to her and almost reach out and touch her.

"If I paint a wild horse, you might not see the horse... but surely you will see the wilderness!"

-Pablo Picasso

It was a transcendent experience which filled him with a relaxed joy, a kind of Powering Down, but also a powerful energy which heightened his visual perception of his surroundings for the rest of the day. For a brief while he learned to see again, just as Vermeer had been able to see.

Powering Down and Powering Up through visual experience is not restricted to the contemplation of man-made imagery. Visions of the physical world can equally provide the same energising effect.

Some years ago, while travelling in Alaska, I joined a group on a helicopter trip to the top of a glacier. The pilot set us down on a remote mountain top. The air was crystal clear, clean and pure, with a bright yellow sun beaming from a deep blue sky. Despite the extreme latitude and high altitude, it was not cold, and all was silent except for the hushed melodic sound of a soft and gently caressing wind.

I stood some distance apart from the others in the group, and as I looked out over the scene I found I could see for miles across distant mountain ranges. I was awe-inspired and felt I never wanted to leave this place. A profound feeling of peace swept over me and I felt myself Powering Down and letting go. It was what I imagined some form of natural heaven would be like. I felt an overwhelming gratitude that I had come to this moment, a gratitude that energised me and Powered me Up and Through to a feeling that life was full of endless possibilities.

We are a highly visual species. The metaphor of vision even leaks into our language – to understand is to 'see'. The emotional impact of visual experiences, the form and composition of a scene, the play of light and shade, can be truly profound, and this is instinctively understood by great artists. If we know what we need, visual experience is a powerful tool for managing our Human Energy.

Light

"It is during our darkest moments that we must focus to see the light"

-Aristotle

Light itself is well known to have important effects on our energy. I love daylight and therefore I love the spring and the summer. I loathe the winter with its low light levels and short daylight hours. In the summer I'm energised, Powered Up by the bright natural daylight. In the autumn and winter I have to rely on Powering Up through the use of artificial light. As a result I've found that I become vespertine, being more energised in the late afternoon and evenings at that time of year. This is ironic since by nature I'm very much diurnal. I now realise the necessity of employing different strategies for managing my Human Energy during different seasons.

This phenomenon is very familiar to those living at high latitudes. Near the Arctic Circle and above, the adverse effects of extended periods of low or absent winter light can present themselves in syndromes such as seasonal affective disorder (SAD). For some this is extremely energy-depleting. It is often treated by utilising special light regimes to bring our natural rhythms back into line. Conversely, long, light summer nights can bring on energy-draining insomnia.

In an ideal world, like some pampered celebrity, I would love to use migration to sunnier climes as my energy management strategy for surviving the autumn and winter months.

However, back to the real world . . .

Colour

"Let me, O let me bathe my soul in colours; let me swallow the sunset and drink the rainbow"

-Kahlil Gibran

Intimately related to vision, colour is another fascinating arena in which to manage Human Energy. Colour has the power to enhance our mood and heal us, rejuvenate us, relax us and stimulate a whole range of different emotions.

The relationship between colour and Human Energy has been the subject of serious investigation for some while. In 1958, the US scientist Robert Gerard conducted a study that claimed to show that red stimulates and makes us anxious, while blue promotes calm. He also showed that colour could affect appetite, blood pressure and aggression, the latter being reduced by the colour pink. This principle has been applied in some US penal institutions where inmates are made to wear pink clothing mainly for the purposes of humiliation, but also in an attempt to reduce aggressive tendencies.

Going back much further, papyrus scrolls dating to 1,550 BCE suggest that the ancient Egyptians used colour to cure certain ailments, while ancient Chinese texts also record the use of colour in a range of therapies. Whether or not these treatments had any real effect we can't know, but it testifies to a long-standing recognition of the importance of colour to human well-being.

Bringing this theme up to date, commercial establishments such as restaurants have not been slow to recognise the significance of the emotional and physiological effects of colour to their bottom line. For example the use of red décor has the general effect of increasing customer's heart rate, making them feel hungrier and wanting to eat quickly – a Power Up and Power Through state ideal for the rapid customer turnover required by fast food establishments.

Similarly, brown tones, which are very earthy, induce feelings of relaxation, comfort and stability – a Power Down state good for coffee shops and bistros where repeat custom is important. Blue on the other hand is to be avoided. Blue is not a colour naturally found in food and can cause loss of appetite. It can however increase thirst, so may be useful in a bar environment.

In the healthcare sector, colour, such as is used in hospital décor, can have a profound effect on the well-being and recovery of patients. This is where sensitivity to the impact of colour on Human Energy can be of major importance. Pure white, although clean, can be seen as too clinical and under-stimulating, causing stress in long-term patients. The most useful colour schemes will depend on the layout and natural lighting of the building, but in general the use of light pastel shades within a limited colour pallet, appears to have the most beneficial effect.

The role of colour as a powerful element of our environment cannot be ignored, and 'colour engineering' is becoming an important part of the design of the built environment.

To make things even more interesting, research suggests that men and women may perceive colour differently, with male colour perception red-shifted slightly towards longer wavelengths, while women are better able to distinguish subtle differences in hue.

Whatever the truth of these gender differences, the subtle and complex impact of colour on our mood and energy should never be underestimated. We should strive to understand how colour affects us personally in terms of the three core energy states, and experiment in using it wherever we can to help achieve optimal energy management.

Creating strategies for our own personal energy management can involve our other senses as well. Let's take for instance the sound of music. Music is another universal language and it has that special amplifying power that causes those that rejoice to rejoice more and those that grieve to grieve more. It reaches you on a profoundly emotional level.

"Without music, life would be a mistake"

-Friedrich Nietzsche

Sound, in the form of music, has long been known to have a deep connection to our innermost emotions. It can transport us in an instant to any event, moment or place in our lives, and often becomes the unconscious soundtrack to our experience of the world.

And it need not be just the sound itself, or the melody, rhythm or beat. It can also be the lyrics or poetry of the song, or any combination of these things, that reaches inside and energises us in different ways.

The sound of different kinds of music has been shown to have specific effects on our body chemistry and therefore our energetic state. Our energy is greatly influenced by an armoury of natural chemicals that our body produces and uses to control and regulate its activity. Music taps into this armoury in very specific ways.

In his book 'Why We Love Music', physicist John Powell explains that relaxing music helps us drop off to sleep because it reduces the amount of Noradrenalin in our system. Noradrenalin conditions our body for active movement and increased energy consumption. In short, relaxing music puts us into a Power Down state, and can help establish a healthy sleep pattern. At the opposite end of the spectrum, loud rhythmic music increases our levels of adrenalin which injects energy, Powers us Up and makes us ready to Power Through. This is why this kind of music is ubiquitously found in the gym and fitness environment.

Our energy state can also be influenced by our sense of smell and taste, although this effect can often be more subtle than that induced by music. We vary enormously in our awareness of and sensitivities to odours and tastes and it is often difficult to predict the energy impact they have on ourselves and others.

Smell and taste are very closely related senses and both rely on the detection of specific chemicals by specially shaped receptors on the tongue and in the olfactory areas in the nose. Unsurprisingly the loss of one of these senses can profoundly impact the other.

Furthermore, both are tightly coupled to our moods and emotional states. Studies using odourless placebo controls have demonstrated that exposure to pleasant fragrances can Power us Up by having a real effect in improving our mood and sense of well-being. In a similar way, unpleasant and intense artificial smells can induce negative emotional responses, draining our energy. Often we may be unaware of the cause of these emotions or the effect they have on our energy state.

Our senses are our only window on the world and the only gateway through which the world can influence our internal energy states. By becoming more aware of this and gaining a better understanding of how these interactions work for us as individuals, our sensory perceptions can become a truly powerful tool in helping us manage our Human Energy to its fullest potential.

Here are some simple guidelines to cultivating your own multi-sensory awareness:

- *Become more aware of what your senses are presenting to you. Take the time to stop and take in the moment. What do you see? What do you hear? What do you feel?*

- *Notice your reaction to the different kinds and levels of light that surround you, so that you can adjust your needs accordingly – particularly on a seasonal basis.*

- *Notice the effects of different colours – which colours tend to Power you Down, which Power you Up and which help to Power you Through. Make a conscious effort to use them to create a supportive colour environment.*

Notice the effects of different styles of music and use them to evoke the desired energy states. Listen to music that Powers you Up to support your ability to Power Through. When you are ready to power Down listen to music that relaxes you and places you in that state.

Become aware of the sensory reactions of others and how these impact their energy. Employ this understanding to manage, modify or mediate your exchanges with them for higher quality interactions.

Chapter 10

Pain – The Silent Thief of Energy

"Can you not hear then the terrible screaming all around you that men call silence?"

-Werner Herzog

It's amazing just how much energy being in pain can consume!

We are physical beings operating in a physical world. As such we must operate within an envelope of acceptable limits. When we exceed those limits we experience pain – this is the body's way of warning us that something is wrong, we are out of our comfort zone and at risk.

Pain is a damage limitation mechanism. It's unpleasant, but that's a good thing. If pain were pleasant we would actively seek it out and would be constantly placing ourselves in danger. Because pain is unpleasant we avoid it and are able to keep ourselves within our safe zone.

However pain is not always helpful but can sometimes be deceptive and lead us to false conclusions, showing up as displacement pain. This type of pain may originate in one body location but present itself in quite another.

Prolonged pain wears us down, draining our energy and sapping our motivation. Eventually, many people with chronic pain develop depression-like symptoms. These include lack of interpersonal interaction, difficulty concentrating on simple tasks, and the desire to simplify their life as much as possible. This often manifests as a desire to seek isolation and quiet. Sleeping often renders the pain less intrusive, and that combined with the exhaustion that pain induces means that it isn't uncommon for a person to start sleeping upwards of ten hours a day.

In the right circumstances however, the three core states of Power Down, Power Up and Power Through can support how we manage our energy to avoid the draining effects of pain and help us return to our natural operating limits.

Pain comes in several varieties, including physical and emotional. We differentiate these types of pain because they manifest in different ways and managing them requires different approaches.

Physical pain

One of my clients, the CEO of a global organisation, enjoys running. His role involves a considerable amount of world travel. He always takes his trainers with him since his daily routine includes a run before breakfast, wherever he is in the world.

These pre-work daily runs were his way of Powering Up to Power Through the day. At the weekends he would also use his running to Power Down. His practice of running was therefore a key tool in the management of his Human Energy.

While engaged in an all-terrain run one weekend he sustained a painful injury to his leg which resulted in him having to abstain from his accustomed early morning runs for a protracted period.

His injury denied him access to the three core states because his running was his primary pathway into those states. After a few weeks he noticed that he was feeling occasional bouts of tiredness. The inflammation from the injury and the resulting nagging background pain was silently sapping his energy. Routine daily tasks seemed to demand more effort than he had been accustomed to.

This is something I identify with from the pain that I endured during the time of my recovery when even the most mundane, normal, everyday activities became challenging.

Tiredness punctuates how we appear and sound to others. Whilst he was enduring his tiredness internally, it was occasionally noticed by some of his colleagues. It even leaked through into the tonality of his voice during a formal business phone call with me.

What he needed was a strategy that could act as a surrogate for his running and re-connect him with the three core states. For him this strategy needed to involve some form of outdoor activity.

He has made time for regular walks with carefully planned workouts at the gym, neither of which activity impacts his injury. Because he has recognised that his energy is important to him, he has actively developed alternative options for reclaiming its management.

Being able to connect with the three core states enables us to reclaim control of our energy and win it back from the clutches of the silent thief that is physical pain.

"Somewhere inside that hurting body, there is something better, something stronger, something real"

-R. M. Drake

Emotional pain

Emotional pain has many different origins, including personal loss, bullying, intimidation, abuse and abandonment.

Emotional pain produces nerviness, anxiety and feelings of hopelessness, but can also manifest itself in physical form such as in headaches, stomach upsets, irritable bowel syndrome (IBS) and chronic pain, which commonly shows up in our neck, back, shoulders, knees and ankles. Emotional pain can therefore physically hurt. It diminishes and compromises our Human Energy, often without our awareness or control.

Unlike physical pain however, emotional pain is not always easy to see, describe or explain, and everyone experiences and deals with it in different ways.

This fact often makes a truly empathetic understanding difficult. We hear phrases like "just get over it" or "stuff happens – deal with it". This attitude is born from a long-embedded notion that emotional pain is somehow less 'real' than physical pain, and can therefore be dismissed as a form of self-indulgence. To me such a view is completely unacceptable. It ignores the fundamental interconnection between the emotions and the physical body. It is equivalent to simply discounting and dismissing another person's reality.

So how do we approach emotional pain?

Too often our lack of emotional self-awareness leads us down a path which is self-destructive. We may employ denial, displacement behaviour or distractions in an attempt to mask the pain-creating issue or situation. By these means we can become acclimatised to the pain, failing to apprehend how far it is diminishing us and chipping away at both our personal identity and our Human Energy.

I can illustrate this process through the experience of a very close friend.

For many years she was trapped in an unhappy marriage. The darkest feature of this period of her life was the fact that she was isolated from all meaningful social community.

During this time her only outlet was through work and study, where at least she had the opportunity to interact with clients, peers, colleagues and associates. She was also blessed with friends who found ways to reach out to her and maintain contact, although at the time she did not realise how important these interactions were to her.

Instead of Powering Down, getting clarity and recognising the source of her unhappiness, my friend compensated by coming to believe the fictitious fantasy that was being created for her, to accept the illusion that she was by nature an introverted, shy and private person, thereby legitimising the situation. She blinded herself to the problem and entered a self-reinforcing downward spiral. Every day she thought she was Powering Through, but in actual fact she was draining her energy and running on empty, most of the time.

The degree to which this experience had sapped my friend's energy and diminished her inner confidence and self-esteem only began to dawn on her some time after the marriage ended.

Left alone with her sons she suddenly found she had a major new set of challenges to face and had to find a way to Power Up to survive. She knew that the first step was to rediscover who she really was.

Throughout the months and years that followed, my friend set out to get re-acquainted with herself. She held up a mirror to the person she had thought she was. What she found was someone else... someone with strength and courage, stamina, resilience, spirit and a *voice*. She grew to like this new person.

"Never bend your head.
Hold it high.
Look the world straight in the eye"

-Helen Keller

My friend began to allow positive energy to flow in from outside and from others, where before she had been afraid to receive it or allow it. Gradually she was Powering Up, and as she did so her confidence returned allowing her to Power Through. This is a road she is still travelling.

If we allow it, pain, both physical and emotional will drain our Human Energy. There are steps we can take to prevent this:

- *Become conscious of the pain and recognise it for what it is.*

- *Where the pain is physical we can look for alternative activities to provide a path back to our three core energy states.*

- *Where the pain is emotional, we should take time out to re-connect with ourselves and engage in activities and human interactions that support us to Power Down and Power Up. For example some may embark on personal development or learning by signing up to educational programmes which provide both a sense of community and purpose.*

Emotional pain is every bit as debilitating as physical pain, but its effects are often harder to see and understand. Although it is not a universal panacea, giving yourself space to apply the idea of the three core states can often shed light in the dark and illuminate the path towards what we might otherwise imagine a stark and forbidding future.

"Look at how a single candle can both defy and define the darkness"

-Anne Frank

Chapter 11

Language – How Energy Speaks

"Conversation should be pleasant without scurrility, witty without affectation, free without indecency, learned without conceitedness, novel without falsehood"

-William Shakespeare

Communication is a phenomenon which is not unique to humans, but the sheer range, depth and subtlety of human communication is found nowhere else in nature.

Human language is a frothing cocktail of words and gestures, meanings and usages, tonality and volume, ambiguity and vocal dexterity. This astonishing capability has the power to energise or de-energise us in the most unseen and subtle ways. How many times have you found yourself agreeing to take on a favour or task, only to find yourself wondering "how the heck did I get roped into that?"

Language is a fine and graceful dance which swirls between our thoughts, senses, and ideas, reaching out beyond our skin to make contact with the world around us.

But language goes well beyond mere sounds shaped into sentences. It's possible to sit in complete silence with someone and hold a conversation while uttering not a single word. We communicate richly through the blink of an eye, a smile, the way we breathe, our posture and our body language. In this way profound meaning and energy may pass silently between us.

In everyday life some forms of silent communication can become ritualised and embedded in the culture. A very good example is the way we greet each other. Ritualised greetings can diminish barriers erected by feelings of social awkwardness through an exchange of Human Energy. A simple handshake preceding a social interaction can either Power us Down and put us at ease, or Power us Up and energise us for the encounter. It is widely understood in business circles that a firm but friendly handshake can break the ice at the beginning of a meeting and temper the negative impact of any ensuing misunderstandings.

Our ability to communicate is so adaptable that we can even compensate for the loss of entire senses. The deaf can communicate visually via sign language. The blind can read through the sense of touch. The urge to communicate is unstoppable.

"The best and most beautiful things in the world cannot be seen or even touched - they must be felt with the heart"

-Helen Keller

Virtually everyone knows someone whose language is so negative that they can walk into a room and evacuate the energy from the building. On the other hand we also know others who inject positive energy into any environment, lighting up the room by their presence alone.

Language is so subtle in the way it affects us and interacts with our energy state that even the same message can either energise us, or demoralise us. For example, the message "we really have a mountain to climb here!" can be seen by some as a positive challenge which inspires and Powers them Up. By others it is received as a dose of negativity which makes them want to give up before they even begin.

Words, and the tone in which they are delivered, can instantly transport us to a new energy state. This can often occur before we realise what is happening. When a stranger barks an order at us to move our car, we instantly feel attacked and we prepare to respond either by rapid withdrawal, frozen inaction or aggressive hostility. The adrenalin begins to flow and our body Powers Up for the confrontation. We want to resist and do the opposite of what is being requested.

On the other hand, if the request is made in a polite and gentle tone, with an accompanying reasoned explanation, we instantly feel calmer, more conciliatory and Powered Down. We are much more disposed to accede to the request.

"Raise your words, not your voice. It is rain that grows flowers, not thunder"

-Rumi

The complexities of language multiply even further. Some see meaning within meaning, a language filled with sub-texts. Those of a cynical disposition will often mistrust even the most pleasant and well-intentioned discourse, reading within it some dark and covert underlying motive. For such people genuinely honest and sincere conversation is rarely credible, and communication is often exhausting and draining for all parties concerned. Nobody wins in this negative Human Energy exchange.

Given all this complexity it's clear that our energy states can be manipulated by the use of language in extremely subtle ways and without our full awareness. It can be done to us, but we can also do it to others. Politicians and salesmen know this only too well and use it to both good, and bad effect.

So how can we use Power Down, Power Up and Power Through to protect ourselves from being helplessly cast adrift on this stormy ocean of language, and avoid having our world crafted for us? How can we use the three core energy states to take back control of language and avoid the emotional manipulation that can hide behind it?

This is not always easy to do.

We can make a start by becoming aware of how the language we routinely use influences our own self-image and energy state. How many times a day do we throw our words away by saying things like, "I'm not good enough", "I hate the way I look," "I'm so stupid," "I'm such a fool." We rarely think that these words bring negative energy and affect us on a physical level, *but they do.* Ancient writings tell us that life and death are in the power of the tongue. As it turns out, that's not just a metaphor.

The more often we say things, the more easily we come to see them as true. Repetition gives birth to belief. Statements we speak, hear or see regularly are more likely to be believed than those we are exposed to only occasionally, regardless of whether or not they are actually true. Once again, politicians, salesmen and brand executives understand this all too well.

In the rapidly evolving world of social media, repetition becomes a synonym for popularity, and popularity becomes a synonym for truth. Gradually the boundary between reality and fantasy dissolves and truth becomes merely what you wish to believe today.

However, opinions are divided between those who see social media as an expansive force for Powering Up and those who regard it as a pernicious energy-draining disease. It may well be changing the way we think about the nature of human relationships and the value of personal privacy versus the value of living an open public life.

Once we start to consider the language we regularly expose ourselves to, we can begin to see how this impacts our self-image and our energy state.

The second thing we can do is become conscious of how our language, and its accompanying subtleties of tone and expression, influences the energy state of those around us.

Our words are tools which can be used to build up or tear down. The right words, spoken in the right way and at the right time, can Power Up a friend, colleague or even a stranger. For example, a simple "well done" or "thank you", a brief and unexpected show of appreciation or gratitude, can make a profound difference to an entire day, and this can also reflect back and Power *us* Up in the process.

Thirdly, we should try to understand how the words of others can shape our own energy state. Being in the company of those who understand the relationship between their use of language and their core energy states can be highly energising. On the other hand, spending time with someone who is constantly negative will have quite the opposite effect. We must choose wisely the people with whom we surround ourselves!

We can attempt to live by a few simple guidelines:

- *We can only do the best we can according to the intelligence and abilities we have been given. Use what words you have to Power Up and create a better self-image. Be kind to yourself and repeat them as often as you can.*

- *When you feel the urge to say something negative, resist it and find a way to say the same thing with positive language. Try to help others Power Up, don't drain their energy.*

- *Seek out and keep the company of those who understand and use these principles. They won't be a drain on your energy and they will make it easy for you to Power Down, Power Up and Power Through.*

Chapter 12

Human Connection - A Universal Essential

Human connection is vital to our physical, emotional and intellectual health. An intimate act, from a simple smile to an affectionate hug, can be contagiously energising to us. This simple act can trigger our 'happy' hormone, serotonin. This is powerful stuff that costs nothing but creates good Human Energy. It's a great way to Power Up.

But without constant attention it can be transient. Intimate energy is like a burning candle. When it's lit, its beautiful flame lights up the room, creating a wonderful ambience with a glowing radiance that sets a scene of tranquillity and warmth with a distinctive scent.

When the candle is blown-out, there is darkness and the wick leaves a wisp of smoke and scent dancing in the air as it cools down. In a short while, the scent and the smoulder will be gone, until we light the candle again.

Intimacy and connection is vital for people of all ages. The parent-child relationship is a prime example of this. Children need the affection of a hug and the feeling of security that it provides. They really thrive in the knowledge that they are loved by their parent/s and family. After all the home is where the heart is. We've all been there as a child and for some of us, also as a parent.

Children often do things for love and attention, but the need for affection is a two-way street. This is where both parents and children can employ the three core states of Human Energy to mutually Power-Up. As parents we also need to know that we are loved and appreciated by our children. This is a relationship which is consistently unpredictable. We cannot always expect displays of affection from our children whenever we want them.

We can however offer them unconditional love and understanding, and prepare the ground by ensuring that we are always available to care for them and support them whenever they want or need it. Children need patience not pressure. We have to have faith that in the long term this will be reciprocated, and sometimes it is, but sometimes we may have to wait a while.

Recently a friend told me of an evening when he and his 37 year-old son were working on a technical problem together. Suddenly his son decided to give him a hug. It came completely out of the blue. This unexpected act at once made him feel that all the years of love, affection and support had been appreciated and acknowledged. This single, simple hug gave him a profound feeling of connection and a brand new energy that left them both Powered Up. They quickly solved their technical problem.

He was not alone. From the moment we're born, we all need hugs.

"A hug is a great gift - one size fits all, and it's easy to exchange"

-Unknown

Dr. Nathalie Maitre of Nationwide Children's Hospital in Columbus, Ohio suggests that touch is absolutely critical for all babies, forming the basis for a lifetime of healthy development, *(Maitre et al., 2017, Current Biology 27, 1–7 April 3, 2017 a 2017 Elsevier Ltd.)*

It's no secret that what doctors and parents are increasingly referring to as kangaroo care, or the simple business of holding babies as much as possible, can have real developmental benefits. Babies who get frequent cuddling tend to sleep better and manage stress more easily. Cuddling Powers them Down.

Think about it for a minute. From the moment we enter this world we are quickly bonded with our birth-giver, creating a special energetic connection that nourishes our inner self – we could refer to it as our spiritual self. This brings meaning to that primary special connection that we are born with.

"We are born of love; love is our mother"

-Rumi

As we become older, our need for intimacy develops into a way of confirming our relationships. But ironically, we also find it harder to be truly intimate. True intimacy requires an openness and willingness to become vulnerable that few people find easy or comfortable.

Nevertheless, intimacy is a significant part of our energy creation, healing and wellbeing processes.

Our innate need for intimacy is not just for the purpose of reproduction. Neither is it an excuse for license, promiscuity or abuse. When intimate energy is in its loving, sensual and spiritual form it is something that connects to our basic human needs in many ways, shapes and shades, physically, intellectually and emotionally.

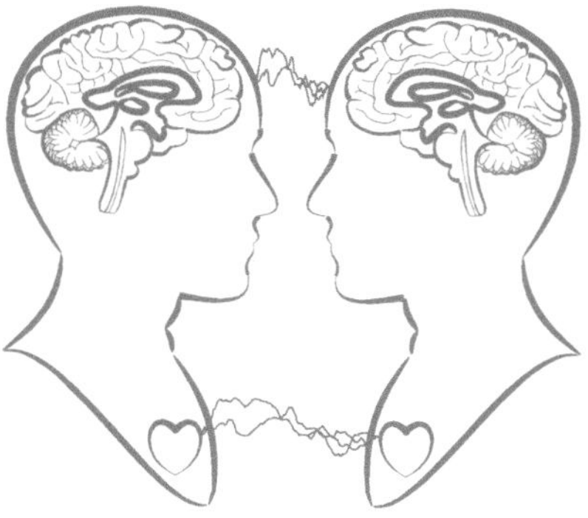

"Physical attraction is common, but mental connection is rare, once you experience the latter, the former is never enough"

-Unknown

Demonstrations of affection can be extremely energising for some people and can trigger a sense of inner peace, calmness and positivity. Intimate energy derives from very personal, emotional, feeling-based connections. Intimacy may be complex but it's no different from other types of energy in that it works well for some and not so well for others. Everyone is different and develops different needs during the course of their life.

The energy we can create from human touch and physical connection can be quite remarkable in its effects. Some people have reported that intimate affection has boosted their immune system, lowered their blood pressure, improved their feeling of wellbeing and added years to their lives.

We know about the importance of eating healthily and taking regular exercise, and how that gives and creates energy for us, but what about the health benefits of intimacy? Lack of intimacy and the emotional imbalance that results can drain our energy in a variety of ways. However, regular displays of genuine affection improve the energetic connection we have with our partner, which will have the effect of Powering Up both.

The emotional imbalance from a lack of intimate affection impacts our health on a much deeper level than we often realise. Physical touch is necessary for whole health. For example, if someone who struggles with overeating comes home from work tired, alone and stressed, what are they likely to do? Head for the biscuit tin, the cakes, crisps, chocolate and beer. You get the idea. But if they come home to a warm, loving partner who hugs them, appreciates them, and desires them, they're much less likely to go for the binge-fix. From a simple smile, to an endearing word, a sensual touch, a hug, a kiss, or physical intimacy, at that moment there is an energy triggered that is key to physical and psychological health.

No matter how many vegetables you eat and how much water you drink, if your emotional energy is out of balance, you will feel neither healthy nor happy.

So, perhaps we could benefit from asking ourselves a few questions:

- *How am I doing in the area of relationships and intimacy?*
- *Could I use some more affection?*
- *How would more affection impact my health and change my life?*
- *What would happen if things stayed the same as they are now?*

Researchers have reported that being appreciated, loved and liked stimulates the release of chemicals such as serotonin and oxytocin which make us feel great and good about ourselves.

With the right partner great intimacy and affection can be an effective and joyful channel for the exchange of energy, even when you may be exhausted. It contributes to a restful sleep, allowing you to Power Down and bounce out of bed in the morning with a glowing radiance that can make the world seem a much better place.

Intimate affection exercised with commitment and without fear or judgement, is one of the most energising experiences available to us.

It can Power us Down and calm us.

It can Power us Up and give us all the strength we need.

It can Power us Through to taking on tasks that would otherwise seem formidable.

Our common experience is that over time, relationships can take on the shape of habits, more of a comfortable and familiar routine than a continuing adventure. If we are not careful it can become a way of merely existing, trapped in a relationship where true intimacy is a distant memory with no recalled purpose or experienced pleasure. Intimacy, like all other expressions of Human Energy, must be carefully nurtured if we are to be able to Power Up with each other in order to Power Through.

The human need to connect does not end within the circle of those close to us. We also crave a wider connection with others, even with those whom we may never even have encountered before.

The gift of giving

There are days when the world can seem like a loveless, empty place, barren of any compassion, care or understanding. We are sometimes left to wonder why, on a planet consisting of billions of human beings, it can still feel so bereft of humanity and humility.

But even on such days we don't have to look far to realise that things are really not quite as bleak as they may seem. There are many examples every day of charitable and philanthropic acts where humans reach out to help each other for no other reason than it is the right and moral thing to do.

"What do we live for if it not to make life less difficult for each other?"

-George Elliot

These selfless acts of giving need not be confined to the actions of individuals. Indeed, many are organised on a global scale, bringing together participants from different countries and even continents. Neither are these acts confined to one-off events, but can also represent continuous giving, such as the activities of groups like Médicins Sans

Frontières who continually risk their lives bringing medical aid into regions scarred by human conflict.

Such activities, from small and local to large and global, all represent a way for individuals to become part of a greater community within which differences can be set aside in the service of a higher, more meaningful purpose.

At the core of all this lies an innate recognition of our common humanity and our need to belong. Charitable and philanthropic acts are specific expressions of this recognition. But it can also come to the surface in the most unexpected places.

A famous example is the Christmas Truce of 1914 in which German and Allied troops left their trenches during an unofficial ceasefire and met in no-man's land to fraternise, talk, exchange food and souvenirs, and even play football together. For a brief moment in time these men overcame their fear of each other, laid down their weapons and found the Human

Energy to Power Down. They ceased to see each other as a nameless, faceless, hostile enemy, but in that moment as fellow human beings sharing the same hopes, joys, fears and privations. One moment these men were trying to kill each other, in the next they were sharing a shot of schnapps. An oasis of human connection in a desert of hostility, created by the power of Human Energy.

This Christmas occurrence has become so culturally iconic of the human need for connection that it has featured in many books, stage plays, on television and in films.

The hierarchy of human needs suggests that the requirement for belongingness, love, intimacy and friendship kicks in once our basic need for food, water, warmth and security have been met. In fact, as the Christmas Truce illustrates, under certain circumstances our need for connection may be so strong that it trumps even some of our basic needs.

In volunteering for acts of charity and philanthropy, as well as simply connecting with others, we are Powering Through and channelling our Human Energy into directed acts of human solidarity. On completion, some will find themselves inspired, energised and Powered Up, while for others the process will leave them calm, satisfied and Powered Down. The effects will be different for each individual.

There are many different ways to satisfy our need for intimacy, or intimate energy. The connectedness we gain from our immediate intimate personal relationships, and the Human Energy that it fosters, can be gained as readily from wider family relationships and even from reaching out to give to strangers.

Here are a few basic ideas that we can use to get started:

- *Aim to exchange at least three smiles per day.*
- *Find ways to commit selfless acts of kindness and giving.*
- *Communicate without judgement and blame.*
- *Practice high quality listening. Resist the burning desire to reply or interrupt with your own opinions.*
- *Arrange regular quality time with those who are important to you.*

Finally, and equally important, is the energy we can gain, or lose, in our daily interactions with those people, groups and teams with whom we spend a vast proportion of our time. We will be explore this in the next chapter.

"Don't walk behind me; I may not lead. Don't walk in front of me; I may not follow. Just walk beside me and be my friend"

-Albert Camus

Chapter 13

Escaping the Treadmill

The majority of us spend most of our waking lives at work. Some of us work alone, but most of us work with others, usually as part of a team.

A team environment is an intense theatre for the interplay of Human Energy, where words, actions, gestures and a myriad other facets of daily human interaction can Power us Down, Power us Up, Power us Through or just exhaust us.

> *"Pleasure in the job puts perfection in the work."*
>
> *-Aristotle*

Sooner or later during our working lives we will all experience both positive and negative team environments. In a positive team things seem to get done with minimum friction. Individuals are clear about who they are, where they are going and the nature and value of their contribution. They feel free to take risks and be creative. They offer each other positive support, help and encouragement, and understand that the team represents something greater than the sum of its individual members.

In such an environment where people commit to each other, Human Energy is amplified, and there is ample opportunity for Powering Down, Powering Up and Powering Through.

A negative team is a different kind of animal. Things get done slowly and painfully, or not at all. There is no clear shared view of identity, direction or goals. People are more committed to their own agendas rather than to the agenda of the group. Individuals are fearful of open cooperation and withdraw into defensive tribes and fiefdoms, relying on satisficing to get them safely through the day. Some people even create conflict because they see opportunity in the resulting confusion which, unfortunately, is interesting, exciting and energising for them.

The point of the day becomes not to be creative, but just to stay on the treadmill and survive. In this environment, Human Energy is drained and wasted.

"If you want to go fast go alone. If you want to go far go together"

-African proverb

What makes the difference between a good and a bad team environment? How do we jump off the treadmill? One major factor is that special kind of Human Energy called leadership.

But what is leadership? What does a leader do that makes the difference?

Browse any bookshop and you will find no shortage of publications offering opinions on the subject. But

I want to look at work, teams and leadership from the perspective of the interplay of Human Energy… how does the energy of a team get created or drained, and what impact can a leader and their energy have on this process?

Whenever you think of a good leader, it's probably true that your image includes someone who demonstrates a significant amount of psychological, emotional, or physical presence.

Of course Human Energy is vital at all levels within a team and some would say that it's even more critical at the leadership level. Being able to tap into that energy even when you are exhausted, or when you're swimming against the tide, often distinguishes good leadership.

A leader uses their energy to provide a single unifying vision to the group where none may have previously existed. This is important because, just as an individual has an identity, a group also needs an identity to make it live.

The identity of the individual tells them who they are in relation to the world. It informs how they may interact and exchange energy with others. It provides them with a past, a present, a future, and a place to which they can belong. Our sense of personal identity may be positive and energising, or negative and draining.

The group identity serves a similar purpose, but for the collective rather than the individual. In a group, individuals substitute part of their personal identity with that of the group. A leader gives shape to the group identity in the form of a vision, and the vision employs and directs the group's Human Energy.

It's a bit like the energy relationship between an orchestra and its conductor. The individual musicians have their instructions in the form of the written score. But it is the conductor who energises and gives purpose to the orchestra through direction, coordination of the musician's playing, and by interpreting and shaping the final sound, pace and character of the piece. The conductor Powers Up the orchestra so that the musicians can act as one, Power Through and deliver the performance.

The shape that a leader gives to the group identity often mirrors their own personal sense of self. Where this is positive, the team identity is also likely to be positive and energising. People will be drawn to such teams and will stay.

Where it is negative or lacking, the team is likely to be dysfunctional, ineffective and energy-draining. Recruitment to such teams will be difficult and team turnover will be high.

People are drawn to and are engaged by a positive attitude and positive energy. The best leaders know this and it's a major reason for leadership success. Good leadership is a force for Powering Up.

It is the responsibility of the leader then, to energise the team and give it an identity, a personality that its members can identify with, be Powered Up by and which provides an environment in which they can easily Power Through to complete tasks.

"I have learned that people will forget what you said, forget what you did, but people will never forget how you made them feel"

-Maya Angelou

But a good leader also knows that the team is a delicate and fickle creature. It is hard to build the energy of a team, but easy to destroy it. For the energy of the team to continue to flourish a leader must do more than simply provide a vision. They must also foster and manage the team's energy on a daily basis.

They must be sensitive to what will create energy for individual team members, what will Power them Up and, of special importance in a productive team setting, what will Power them Through.

"Courage is what it takes to stand up and speak. Courage is also what it takes to sit down and listen"

-Winston Churchill

For example, a leader may need to understand when best to re-assign an individual from one project or task to another. For some, coming to the end of a project may be a Power Down event. This is a kind of relief energy, following the sustained effort and focus of a long and concentrated set of tasks.

For others, the event may have a Power Up effect with the excitement gained from the anticipation of engagement with something new. There will also be a few who may be de-energised at the thought of an ending of something familiar, and of facing new and unknown challenges.

Any kind of change or transformation requires considerable amounts of Human Energy. This will have different effects on different people and a key component of leadership is to understand these nuances, and when to challenge them, as a means of nurturing the collective Human Energy of the team. A decision made with sensitivity can be empowering to the individual and the team. An insensitive decision can easily have the opposite effect.

"True leadership stems from individuality that is honestly and sometimes imperfectly expressed... Leaders should strive for authenticity over perfection"

-Sheryl Sandberg

Leadership is a complex creature, but it's not the only source of energy needed to create a highly motivated team environment. Interactions between team members can be equally important in setting the level and nature of Human Energy within the group.

Each individual is affected by the daily events around them. Whether you're working remotely or in a busy office, just one negative phone call from a boss, colleague or client can put a dampener on your day and deplete your energy.

On the other hand, a good call or positive interaction is enough to Power you Up and give you the energy resource you need to Power Through and deliver.

Changes in your core energy state will in turn impact the energy of those you interact with, running like a cascade through the team. Energy, both positive and negative, within a close working group is infectious. Anything that you can do to help others to Power Up and Power Through is a good investment in your own wellbeing.

A powerful way for team members to increase each other's energy and the energy of the group is through the recognition, celebration and rewarding of success.

Recognising, celebrating and rewarding successes, even small ones, is highly energy-generating. How do you feel when you complete a challenging task? How do you feel when you win something or when you sell something? You feel a sense of accomplishment which is highly energising in itself. But that energy is amplified when others in your team also recognise your achievement. It solidifies your sense of self and your identification with the group. It Powers you Up and potentiates you to Power Through.

Acknowledgement and recognition is extremely important for most of us, irrespective of age, gender, race or culture. At some level, most of us just need a little recognition, a little "well-done" or "thank you", to feel validated and energised.

In fact, whilst I was immersed in my research for my Master's degree, I discovered that recognition was more important to people than receiving actual rewards. Furthermore, when rewards were given they became more meaningful to the person when combined with recognition. The recognition seems to be necessary to connect us to the value of the reward and have it energise us and Power us Up to do better and achieve even higher standards. Reward without the accompanying expression of *authentic* recognition is ephemeral and its energy is soon gone, like a wisp of vapour.

Good quality celebration of success must incorporate good quality recognition. Taking time to celebrate puts a landmark in your timeline and sets a benchmark for going forward, to embrace the next challenge and achieve that new set of goals. It sets up a positive feedback loop which can energise the whole team environment.

All these strategies foster a positive, enthusiastic, energised working environment where individuals are Powered Up by the team. The pay-off is that in such an environment people will simply get more done.

It may even be the case that the recent trend towards coffee-shop working and meetings, could be more about placing ourselves in a buzzing, energetic environment that helps us Power Through, than about the coffee itself.

So if we are trapped on the daily treadmill, what can we do to escape?

When we find ourselves in a negative environment, running fast and getting nowhere, escape from the treadmill need not be that difficult.

Where inspiring leadership is absent, we can set the process in motion by taking matters into our own hands and actively recognising and celebrating the successes, large and small, of those around us.

We can begin to make our colleagues feel that they are valued, that their contributions matter and that they are part of something positive and larger than themselves.

A group sense of identity and a team energy will gradually emerge which will in turn Power Up those around us in a virtuous cycle, leading to yet more positive energy. Small, purposeful, co-operative groups will begin to develop and as this spreads, so will the development of informal direction and vision, in the service of which people will willingly Power Through.

"Great things in business are never done by one person.
They are done by a team of people"
-Steve Jobs

Here are some basic ideas for fostering a higher quality and positive sense of team energy.

- *Leadership energy needs to be directed towards supporting and empowering, not controlling and restricting, to cultivate high quality team energy.*

- *Rewards must be accompanied with appreciative and authentic recognition to create more Power Up energy.*

- *Avoid creating negative emotional states through energy-draining criticism. Instead, promote, encourage and exchange positive and constructive communication and feedback.*

Summary

Some Final Thoughts

The Universe is filled with energy. The long-established Law of the Conservation of Energy teaches us that this energy can neither be added to nor subtracted from. But it *can* be converted from one form into another. Within this conversion process lies the possibility to put the energy to useful work – to bring about some physical change in the world.

Human Energy is no exception. We have a limited amount of the stuff. We derive our energy from our nutrition, and ultimately, we lose it to the environment as heat. But while we have it, we can transform it from one form into another and in so doing benefit our own lives and the lives of others.

At the beginning of this book I introduced the idea of the three core energy states

Power Down,

Power Up,

Power Through.

These are simply convenient labels for the basic conceptual forms in which we hold our Human Energy. In the Power Down state we are holding it in storage, controlled, organised and ready to be made available. In the Power Up state we are taking it out of storage and heating it up, making it ready to do work. In the Power Through state we are expending that prepared energy to actively direct some form of transformation in the world.

The very existence of these three states was the first idea I wanted to introduce. The second and equally important idea in this book is that *when* and *how* we *transition* between these three states need not be a matter of chance, but something that can be brought under our own control. Life need not be something that is 'done to us', but something that we can control and direct for ourselves.

"Managing and using the three core energy states is a great way of 'showing up' for your own life"

Throughout this short book I have tried to provide a feeling for the surprising and astonishing complexity of factors that influence our energy state. Much of this is based on published scientific research, some on my own experiences, and some on the feedback I have had from others during my career in personal development. In the space available I have only been able to scratch the surface, and there remain many areas I would like to explore further.

At first sight this sheer complexity may seem to indicate that we are no more than unwitting actors in our own lives, bound by a script we can barely hope to understand, much less alter. Many try to escape this dilemma by the use of external stimuli to force transitions between their energy states, but they are missing the point.

I hope that within these pages I have seeded the idea that this apparent complexity is illusory. We can boil it down, tame it and bring it under control simply by realising that our Human Energy is ours to dispose of as we will. This is a form of liberation. And key to this realisation are the three core energy states which provide the vehicle for enacting that new liberty.

The three core states are places you can *choose* to be. You can place yourself in any one of them through a variety of means. I have given examples of some of these means within this book, but everyone is different and you will need to discover which paths best suit you.

Mastering the power of human energy is more than just an acquired skill; it is a work of art as well as a way of thinking, doing and being. It becomes a way of life.

A better understanding and respect for the power of Human Energy would provide us with a more realistic perspective on the world and on our issues and challenges.

The first step to mastering your own Human Energy is to ask yourself a few basic questions:

- *What do the concepts of Power Down, Power Up and Power Through look like in the context of my life?*

- *How do I get energised? What elements of my life will be most effective in helping me achieve each of these states (e.g. recognition at work, family and friends, a good night's sleep, colours, music and singing, walking and travel, reading and films, food, drink and laughter)*

- *In what ways do I routinely misdirect and waste my Human Energy?*

- *In what ways are others misdirecting their Human Energy at me?*

- *What will I do next?*

As you begin to answer these questions, and translate the answers into daily practice, you will come to a better understanding of when you need to Power Down, Power Up and Power Through, and the means to get there.

Human Energy is the currency of our lives. We should all strive to be more openly conscious and mindful of how we manage it and choose to expend it, of how it impacts us and how it impacts others.

I wrote this book with the heartfelt intention that it should be a helpful beginner's guide to Human Energy management; a place to start and a springboard from which to reach out and discover more. It is not intended as a formal academic or scientific work but as a catalyst for personal reflection, to help you unlock, manage and control the energy that you need.

Please take from it what you will and, most of all, enjoy the journey.

Today you are You

That is truer than true

There is no one alive

That is Youer than You

-Dr Seuss

Kindest wishes, Kala

Lightning Source UK Ltd.
Milton Keynes UK
UKHW050714200319
339510UK00007B/107/P

9 781999 645588